MISSOURI

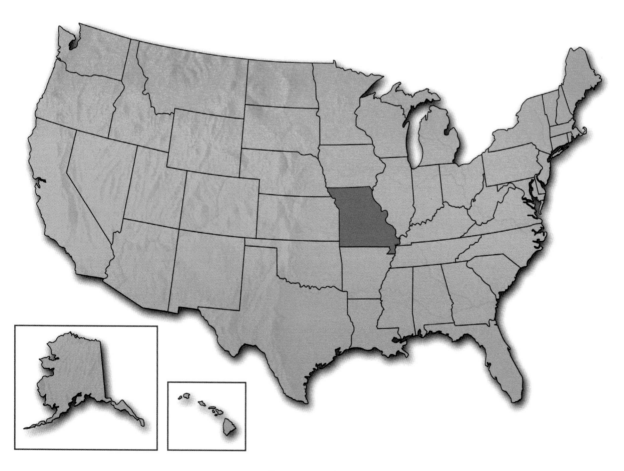

Natasha Evdokimoff

Published by Weigl Publishers Inc.
123 South Broad Street, Box 227
Mankato, MN   56002
USA
Web site: http://www.weigl.com
Copyright © 2002 WEIGL PUBLISHERS INC.

Library of Congress Cataloging-in-Publication Data

Evdokimoff, Natasha.
    Missouri / Natasha Evdokimoff.
        p. cm. -- (A kid's guide to American states)
    Includes index.
    ISBN 1-930954-43-3
      1. Missouri--Juvenile literature. [1. Missouri.] I. Title. II. Series.

F466.3 .E94 2001
977.8--dc21

2001026140

ISBN 1-930954-86-7 (pbk.)

Printed in the United States of America
1 2 3 4 5 6 7 8 9 10   05 04 03 02 01

Project Coordinator
Michael Lowry
Substantive Editor
Rennay Craats
Designers
Warren Clark
Terry Paulhus
Layout
Susan Kenyon
Photo Researcher
Diana Marshall

Photograph Credits

Every reasonable effort has been made to trace ownership and to obtain permission to reprint copyright material. The publishers would be pleased to have any errors or omissions brought to their attention so that they may be corrected in subsequent printings.

Cover: Becky Thatcher look-alike (© Buddy Mays/CORBIS), brass jazz instruments (EyeWire, Inc.); **Scott Barrow:** page 13T; **City of Independence:** pages 6BR, 21BR, 23BL; **Convention and Visitors Bureau of Greater Kansas City:** pages 3B, 7BR, 20T, 23T, 23BR, 26T, 26BL, 29B; **Corbis Corporation:** pages 12T, 15T, 27B; **Corel Corporation:** pages 3M, 4T, 10BL, 11B, 13B; **Fair Saint Louis/Tom Farnam:** page 25T; **Gateway Arch and Museum of Western Expansion:** pages 6T, 12BR; **Hannibal Convention & Visitors Bureau:** pages 3T, 7T, 22B, 25B; **Hermann Tourism Group:** page 22T; **Lambert-St. Louis International Airport/City of St. Louis Airport Authority:** page 5T; **Lampo Communications:** page 29T; **Missouri Department of Natural Resources photo:** pages 8B, 9T, 9BR, 10T, 10BR, 11T, 14T, 14BL, 15B, 27T; **Missouri Division of Tourism:** pages 4BL, 5BL, 6BL, 7BL, 9BL, 21T, 21BL; **Steve Mulligan Photography:** page 8T; © **A. Pichette/Bruce Bennett Studios:** page 26BR; **PhotoDisc, Inc.:** pages 20BL, 28B; **Photofest:** pages 24BL, 24BR; **Susan Spetz/The Image Finders:** page 14BR; **Used by permission, State Historical Society of Missouri, Columbia:** pages 16T, 16B, 17T, 17BL, 17BR, 18T, 18B, 19T, 19BL, 19BR; © **Walt Disney Pictures/Photofest:** page 28T; **Andrea Wells:** page 12BL; **Randy Wells:** pages 4BR, 24T.

CONTENTS

There are approximately 110,000 farms in Missouri, the second-largest number in the country after Texas.

INTRODUCTION

Missouri takes its name from the river that flows through it. It is an Algonquian name and it means "town of the large canoes." Today, Missouri is known as "The Show Me State." The nickname is thought to have come from Congressman Willard Vandiver in 1899. It represents an attitude of common sense among the people. For Vandiver, who was not impressed by talk, actions spoke louder than words.

Missouri is often called "The Center State," because of its location at the heart of the nation. The state shares many characteristics with its neighboring states. Its grainfields and cornfields are reminders of the Midwest, while its cotton fields reflect the South. Missouri's cattle ranches are a fond reminder of the West, and the state's manufacturing factories recall those found in the East.

QUICK FACTS

Kansas City calls itself "The Heart of America." Out of all the large cities in the United States, it is the closest to the center of the country.

Missouri was the twenty-fourth state to enter the Union, on August 10, 1821.

The state flower is the hawthorn blossom. Early settlers made jelly using hawthorn berries.

More than 7.2 million visitors travel to St. Louis every year.

The Lambert-St. Louis International Airport serves about 30 million passengers every year.

QUICK FACTS

The state bird, the bluebird, is a symbol of happiness.

The Missouri mule is the state animal. The mule's toughness made it popular with early farmers.

St. Louis is the largest inland **riverport** in the country.

The fiddle is the official state instrument. The fiddle was the main source of musical entertainment for early settlers.

Getting There

Missouri is bordered to the south by Arkansas, to the west by Oklahoma, Kansas, and Nebraska, and to the north by Iowa. The great Mississippi River forms the state's eastern border with Illinois, Kentucky, and Tennessee.

The **confluence** of the Mississippi and Missouri Rivers, near St. Louis, is an important transportation crossroads. Early traffic on the two rivers brought settlers and traders into the region. Today, Missouri has more than 122,800 miles of public highway linking it to the rest of the country. Missouri also has 489 airports to serve air travelers. Most of these are private airfields. St. Louis and Kansas City are home to the state's main public airports. Railroads also play an important role in transporting goods throughout the state and to other parts of the country. The state is crisscrossed by 4,390 miles of track.

Missouri Location Map

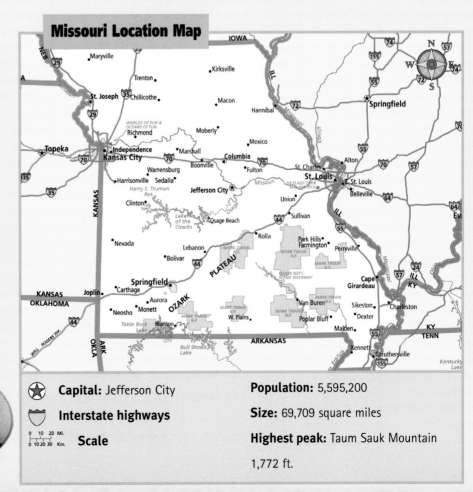

Capital: Jefferson City

Interstate highways

Scale

Population: 5,595,200

Size: 69,709 square miles

Highest peak: Taum Sauk Mountain 1,772 ft.

The Museum of Westward Expansion tells the story of Missouri's historic role in the settlement of the West.

Missouri was the starting point for many important journeys westward. In 1804, explorers Meriwether Lewis and William Clark began their great voyage of discovery from St. Louis. The Lewis and Clark expedition led the way for trade and settlement in the West. Until 1845, Missouri was the nation's westernmost state and was known as the "gateway to the west." Many pioneers traveled through Missouri on their way to California and Oregon.

In 1860, the eastern starting point of the Pony Express was established in St. Joseph. The Pony Express delivered mail from Missouri to California using a series of horses and riders. Both the Sante Fe and Oregon Trails also began in Missouri. These trails provided routes for the movement of people and goods to and from the West Coast.

QUICK FACTS

Missouri Day is held every year on the third Wednesday in October.

The state fish is the channel catfish.

The state insect is the honeybee.

The official state song is the "Missouri Waltz."

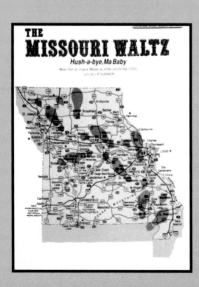

The Sante Fe and Oregon Trails, which start at Independence, Missouri, were two of the principal trails that led settlers and traders from east to west across the United States.

The figure of Tom Sawyer comes from Mark Twain's popular novels. Twain was born and raised in Missouri.

QUICK FACTS

The square dance is the official state dance.

Missouri's state motto is "The Welfare of the People Shall Be the Supreme Law."

The most destructive tornado in the country's history happened in Annapolis on March 18, 1925. It left a 980-foot-wide trail and demolished the town. Nearly 3,000 people were injured and 823 people were killed.

The official state flag was declared on March 22, 1913.

In the twentieth century, Missouri was a place of cultural innovation. In the 1920s, large cities like St. Louis and Kansas City made important contributions to both jazz and blues music. Kansas City is often referred to as the mother of **swing** and **bebop**. These two styles of jazz music emerged from Kansas City's nightclubs and influenced jazz culture for generations. St. Louis's contribution to music history came in the form of the blues. "St. Louis Blues" is one of the most well-known blues songs of all time.

In the later half of the century, Missouri's schools and communities struggled with racial **segregation**, while severe air and water pollution forced the state to spend millions of dollars on environmental cleanups. Today, changes to the educational system, tough environmental controls, and a healthy economy are helping Missourians look to a bright future.

Kansas City jazz clubs are known around the world for creating new jazz sounds.

Ha Ha Tonka State Park is a geological wonder, with sinkholes, caves, and distinct rock formations.

QUICK FACTS

Warsaw holds the record for the highest temperature ever recorded in the state. It reached 118°F on July 14, 1954.

Missouri is divided into three land areas—the Central Lowland, the Ozark Plateau, and the Gulf Coastal Plain.

One of the largest bodies of water in Missouri is the Lake of the Ozarks. It is 125 miles long and has about 1,300 miles of shoreline.

LAND AND CLIMATE

Missouri's landscape is a combination of rolling hills, deep valleys, lush forests, and plentiful farmland. There are even some mountains in the south that rise up to more than 1,700 feet. While not high compared to other ranges, these mountains create a beautiful contrast to the rest of Missouri.

The weather in Missouri is often unstable. Tornadoes occur an average of twenty-seven times a year. Temperatures in the summer can reach as high as 100° Fahrenheit, and July averages are between 76°F and 80°F. Hot summer months often bring thunderstorms and heavy rain. The southeast corner of the state receives the most rain, averaging 50 inches per year. Winter temperatures can be as cold as 16°F in some areas. Winter averages in Missouri are between 36°F and 38°F. The high northern parts of the state receive the most snow. Between 10 and 20 inches of powdery snow fall on Missouri each year.

The Missouri River flows east, from Kansas City to St. Louis, where it joins the Mississippi River.

NATURAL RESOURCES

Trees cover about one-third of Missouri. Oak, walnut, and red cedar trees are found across the state. Forestry is an important business in the state with lumber, flooring, and railroad ties as the key wood products.

The state is also rich in minerals. More lead is produced in Missouri than in any other state. Lime, coal, barite, zinc, and iron ore are also mined. Missouri is a leading state in zinc and lime production. Minerals mined in Missouri are sold across the country. Other resources, including oil, are found in smaller quantities.

The Bollinger Mill State Historic Site represents almost 200 years of milling history. Here, visitors can observe corn being ground by water power.

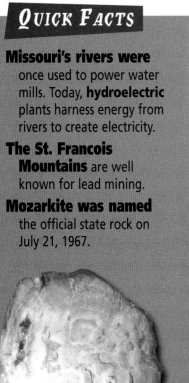

QUICK FACTS

Missouri's rivers were once used to power water mills. Today, **hydroelectric** plants harness energy from rivers to create electricity.

The St. Francois Mountains are well known for lead mining.

Mozarkite was named the official state rock on July 21, 1967.

Missouri's three leading mineral products are lead, portland cement, and crushed stone.

Violets are hardy plants that bloom in early spring. They are commonly found in the Ozark Mountains.

PLANTS AND ANIMALS

Spring is a welcomed time in Missouri. Some flowers, such as the spring beauty, bloom as early as the end of February. Missouri is home to more than 3,200 different species of plants. The state has several native plants, including the Missouri evening primrose, the cream wild indigo, and the Missouri coneflower. Flowers common to the state include violets, buttercups, and wild roses. Many wildflowers line Missouri's roadsides, including Queen Anne's lace, black-eyed Susan, blazing star, and wild sweet William. Wild grape, ivy, and honeysuckle are three of the state's leafy vines. Bluegrass can be found throughout Missouri, although it is not native to the area.

QUICK FACTS

The Mark Twain National Forest is a hot spot for bird-watchers.

Protecting the environment is a top priority in Missouri. State programs guard **ecosystems** in all regions of the state.

Missouri's conservationists are always on the lookout for plant poachers. Poachers steal certain plants from public and private property to use in herbal medicines.

The flowering dogwood, Missouri's state tree, rarely grows over 40 feet, and is known for its tiny flowers of four white petals.

By 1890, the white-tailed deer was nearly extinct in Missouri. In 1944, deer populations were reported to have increased to about 15,000, due to conservation programs.

About seventy species of mammals live in Missouri's forests and hills. Smaller mammals in the state include rabbits, woodchucks, minks, and opossums. Larger mammals such as white-tailed deer, black bears, and mountain lions can also be found. Six species of animals have disappeared from Missouri—the gray wolf, the red wolf, the white-tailed jackrabbit, the Ozark big-eared bat, the buffalo, and the elk.

For bird-watchers, Missouri is an ideal location. Robins, bluebirds, cardinals, doves, and hawks grace the sky. Bass, pike, perch, and catfish provide good fishing in state waters. Hikers should be careful of poisonous rattlesnakes and copperhead snakes that are found in the hills.

The Missouri Department of Conservation works to protect and conserve the state's wildlife and natural resources. Every month, the department holds events to educate the public about dangers to the environment, and what they can do to help.

QUICK FACTS

Black bears once roamed the state's forests in large numbers, but were hunted to near **extinction** for their fur.

The Missouri Department of Conservation is attempting to re-introduce elk to the state.

Meadowlarks, owls, and orioles can all be found in Missouri.

Missouri's owl population is in decline, as a result of pollution and the disappearance of their habitat.

The Lake of the Ozarks is a popular destination for wakeboarders, water-skiers, swimmers, and boaters.

QUICK FACTS

Jesse James, the well-known old-west bandit, was born in Missouri in 1847. People can visit the home where he died in St. Joseph.

Fans of literature will want to visit Hannibal, Mark Twain's boyhood home.

The Climatron Conservatory, in St. Louis, is both a National Historic Landmark and a site for leading scientific research. Visitors can enter the **geodesic dome**, which was built by inventor R. Buckminster Fuller in 1947.

TOURISM

Missouri's outdoors are a popular destination for vacationers from across the country. The scenic Ozark Mountains are found in the west, just south of the Missouri River. The Ozarks offer canyons, caves, and lush forests. The Bagnell Dam on the Osage River has created the Lake of the Ozarks. The lake is one of the world's largest **reservoirs.** It stretches for 92 miles from one end to the other. The lake is home to a variety of activities, including golfing and camping. More than 3 million people visit the Lake of the Ozarks each year.

The Gateway Arch in St. Louis is another popular tourist attraction. The arch is a symbol of the city's role in the country's westward expansion. Every year, over 1 million visitors take the tram ride to the top of this 630-foot-tall structure. It is the tallest national monument in the country.

The Gateway Arch is more than twice as tall as the Statue of Liberty.

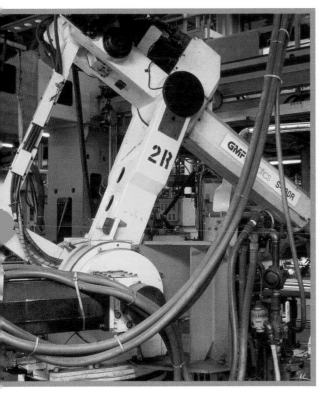

St. Louis is an automobile manufacturing center. Ford, Chrysler, and General Motors all have plants in the city.

INDUSTRY

Missouri is known as a manufacturing state. More than $40 billion is earned through the sale of manufactured goods every year. Transportation equipment such as cars, trucks, and airplanes are manufactured in the state. Missouri also has a food-processing industry which produces soft drinks, flour, meats, and canned fruits. Other Missouri made products include soaps, detergents, missiles, and chemicals for farming and for medicines.

Kansas City and St. Louis are the major manufacturing centers in Missouri. Kansas City's location near the plains makes it a perfect place for agricultural processing. In St. Louis, the industries are mostly mechanical. Automobile assembly and **aerospace** technology make St. Louis a high-technology center. The Anheuser-Busch company, in St. Louis, is the world's largest brewer. The company operates twelve breweries across the United States.

Missouri's grape and wine industry is nearly 150 years old. The state's wineries attract more than 2.5 million visitors each year.

More than 300 varieties of soybean are marketed in the state of Missouri.

GOODS AND SERVICES

Farms in Missouri produce a variety of fresh goods. Primary Missouri crops include hay, corn, oat, rice, and tobacco. Much of the state's corn and hay is used to feed livestock. Cotton, rice, soybeans, and wheat grow well in southeast Missouri. Soybeans are the state's most valuable crop. In recent years, more than 5 million acres of land have been planted with soybeans in Missouri.

In the north, the land is too rugged for crops, but it is ideal for raising livestock. The sale of meat contributes more than $2.4 billion to Missouri's economy. Beef and pork products are produced in the northern part of the state. Large livestock farms raise cows and hogs. In some areas, cows and hogs outnumber people. Other meat and dairy goods include turkey, milk, and eggs. Dairy farming is common in southwestern Missouri.

There are more than 4.4 million cows in Missouri.

The Boeing Company employs approximately 16,400 people in Missouri.

Transportation and aerospace equipment is also produced in the state. The McDonnell Douglas Corporation was once a major producer of jet fighters, commercial aircrafts, and space vehicles. The company was formed in the 1960s, and was one of Missouri's largest employers. In 1997, the McDonnell Douglas Corporation was purchased by the Boeing Company.

The service industry also contributes greatly to the state's economy. More people work in service jobs than in any other area of work. Service employees in Missouri work in hotels, restaurants, and stores. There are about 2.8 million people employed in Missouri. The wholesale and retail trade industry employs about 560,000 people, while manufacturing employs an additional 364,000.

QUICK FACTS

One of Missouri's best-known hydroelectric plants is the Bagnell Dam. It provides electricity to the St. Louis area. Other dams generating hydroelectricity include the Iowa, the Keokuk, and the Taum Sauk.

The McDonnell Douglas Corporation was formed when two aerospace companies **merged** in 1967. The two companies were the Douglas Aircraft Company and the McDonnell Aircraft Corporation.

The McDonnell Aircraft Corporation was founded by James Smith McDonnell in St. Louis in 1939. By the 1960s, the company was the largest employer in Missouri and the leading producer of jet fighters in the country.

The construction of the Bagnell Dam provided more than 20,500 Missourians with jobs from 1929 until its completion in 1931.

FIRST NATIONS

The Osage spoke the Siouan language. They occupied a large area between the Missouri and Arkansas Rivers.

Early hunters, called Paleo-Indians, inhabited the Missouri region as long as 12,000 years ago. The Paleo-Indians were followed by the Woodland culture, and then the Mound Builders. The Mound Builders were so named for the large mounds of dirt that they left behind. It is believed that these mounds served as burial sites and places of worship.

By the seventeenth century, the Osage, the Crow, the Missouri, the Iowa, the Blackfoot, and the Sioux had settled in villages along the Missouri River valley. The area contained bison and other wild animals that were hunted for food. Fish were plentiful in the nearby river. Animal skins were used for shelter and clothing. Some nations farmed Missouri's **fertile** land. By the 1830s, most of Missouri's Native Peoples had been driven out of the state by European settlement. Many Native Peoples were moved to **reservations** in Oklahoma.

QUICK FACTS

The Mound Builders are thought to have lived in Missouri around 800 AD. They are believed to be the ancestors of today's Native Americans.

In the seventeenth century, the Osage first encountered French explorers near the Osage River, in present-day Missouri. The Osage were the largest group of Native Americans in the Missouri area.

Missouri's Native Peoples lived almost half of the year in settled villages. The remainder of the year was spent on the move, hunting game.

Once the crops were planted near their villages, the Osage went on long hunting trips, which lasted most of the spring and summer.

Fur-trapping parties were often sent from St. Louis to the West to trade fur with the First Nations. These were called "summer rendezvous."

EXPLORERS AND MISSIONARIES

The first Europeans to set foot on Missouri land were French trappers and missionaries. In 1673, Father Jacques Marquette and explorer Louis Joliet sailed down the Mississippi River, and charted the land that would become Missouri. Later, in 1682, René-Robert Cavelier, Sieur de La Salle, claimed the entire Mississippi **drainage basin**, including Missouri, for France.

In the years following Cavelier's voyage, French trappers, traders, and missionaries moved into the Missouri region. In 1700, missionaries established the first European settlement in Missouri—the Mission of St. Francis Xavier. The site of the mission was poorly chosen. It was located near several swamps and as a result was abandoned three years later. It was not until about 1750 that Missouri received its first permanent European settlement at Ste. Genevieve.

Father Marquette came to North America, from France, to convert Native Americans to Christianity.

French fur trader Pierre Laclède was sent from New Orleans to establish a trading post near the Missouri River.

EARLY SETTLERS

In 1763, French fur trader Pierre Laclède and his group chose St. Louis to be their trading post. They began clearing the land to build their village. Only a few months later, they learned that France had given the area to Spain. Don Pedro Piernas arrived in 1770 from Spain and made St. Louis the capital of Upper Louisiana.

After the United States took control of the Illinois region, French settlers from Illinois began moving to Missouri. The Spanish governor encouraged this, offering free land to anyone who would settle there. Between 1795 and 1803, hundreds of settlers from Kentucky, Tennessee, the Virginias, and the Carolinas flocked to Missouri to take advantage of the free land. While the newly formed United States territories discouraged slavery in the North, the Spanish welcomed it, drawing in settlers from the South.

The site of St. Louis was chosen because it was close to the Missouri River, but far enough away that it was protected from floods.

During the American Civil War, the city of St. Louis was placed under martial law.

By 1804, there were more than 10,000 people living in Missouri. Most early settlers came from European countries. People arrived from France, Spain, England, Ireland, and Germany to live in the area. Europeans settled mostly in towns in the hope of finding jobs. Settlers from neighboring states also came to Missouri. Steamboats along the Missouri and Mississippi Rivers transported settlers to the state from around the country.

Missourians were divided over whether or not slavery should be allowed. The debate was held across the country. Many northern states pushed for an end to slavery, while the southern states were prepared to fight for the right to keep slaves. As a result, the American Civil War erupted in 1861 when many southern states left the Union to form the Confederate States of America. While many Missourians served with the Confederacy, the state of Missouri remained a part of the Union during the conflict. At the end of the war, slavery was **abolished**.

QUICK FACTS

Well-known pioneer Daniel Boone settled near St. Louis in 1799. He served as a frontier judge in the Femme Osage region of St. Charles.

On June 4, 1812, the United States government declared Missouri a territory.

In 1857, one of the most controversial court cases over slavery was held in Missouri. The United States Supreme Court ruled that Dred Scott, a slave from Missouri, was not a free man.

Steamboat traffic grew rapidly with westward expansion. The construction of steamboats in St. Louis began in the mid-1800s.

Kansas City covers parts of four counties—Jackson, Clay, Platte and Cass.

POPULATION

Missouri's growth rate is slightly higher than that of most of the surrounding states. Today, more than 5.5 million people live in the state. If the population was evenly spread, there would be about 79 people for every square mile of land. Due to the rugged **terrain**, the Ozark region is less populated than the rest of state.

Kansas City is Missouri's most populated center. The city is located next to Kansas City, Kansas. There are no natural boundaries dividing these two cities. Around 440,000 people live on the Missouri side, and more than 140,000 live on the Kansas side. St. Louis is the next highest city in population, with about 340,000 residents. Springfield, Independence, and Columbia are other large cities in the state.

Missouri Cultural Groups

85%	☐ European Heritage
11%	■ African American
2%	☐ Hispanic American
1%	☐ Native American
1%	■ Asian American

The beautiful State Capitol, in Jefferson City, was completed in 1917.

QUICK FACTS

Missouri's state seal was adopted on January 11, 1822. It was designed by Judge Robert William Wells.

There are two Missourians in the United States Senate and nine in the House of Representatives.

The Supreme Court of Missouri is the state's highest court of law.

There are three branches of government in Missouri—the executive, the legislative, and the judicial.

POLITICS AND GOVERNMENT

Missouri's present constitution was written in 1945. It is the state's fourth constitution since joining the Union in 1821. Any **amendments** to the constitution must be approved by the majority of voters.

Governors serve four-year terms. A governor can serve up to two terms in a row and then must step down. The Missouri House of Representatives has 163 members, while the Senate has 34 members. These two groups make up the state's General Assembly, which creates new laws. Missouri has a total of eleven electoral votes in federal elections.

Cities and counties play an important role in state politics. Missouri was the first state in the country to allow its cities to have their own governing **charters**. There are 114 counties in the state, plus St. Louis. The city of St. Louis is considered its own county.

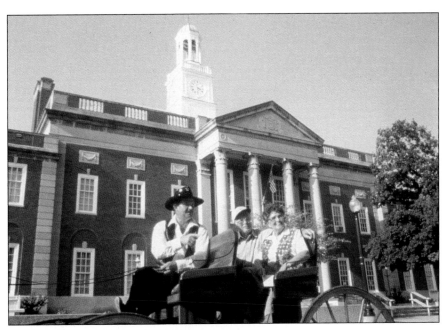

The Independence Square Courthouse contains the restored office and courtroom that President Harry S. Truman once occupied as county judge in 1933.

Hermann was built in 1836 by German settlers. This town celebrates its distinct German heritage in the annual Oktoberfest.

CULTURAL GROUPS

Missouri's rich heritage provides for a wealth of cultural activity. Many Native-American and European traditions are celebrated across the state. The Ozark region has a strong folk-story tradition. Folk tales are told to large gatherings of eager listeners. Folk music, dancing, food, and crafts are also celebrated in festivals around the state. Homemade funnel cakes are a popular folk snack. Square dancing and clog dancing are performed while musicians play folk instruments. Fiddles, banjos, harmonicas, spoons, and mouthbows combine to create the traditional sounds of folk music. Many folk groups play a style of music called **bluegrass**.

European settlers brought their own traditions to Missouri. The large German population hosts many annual festivals, such as Oktoberfest in the fall. Bratwurst sausage, sauerkraut, and delicate strudel pastries are served. Missourians dance the German polka to accordion and **autoharp** music.

QUICK FACTS

Max Hunter, a traveling salesman from Missouri, recorded about 1,600 folk songs from the Ozark Mountains.

Missouri's Irish Americans are known for step dancing. Dancers wear special hard-soled shoes and bright-green Celtic costumes. A traditional Irish dance is called a "*ceilidh.*"

Lederhosen are a pair of short pants with suspenders. This traditional German costume is worn for Oktoberfest celebrations.

On October 17th and 18th, Hannibal hosts the Autumn Historic Folk-life Festival, where artisans demonstrate crafts from the mid-1800s.

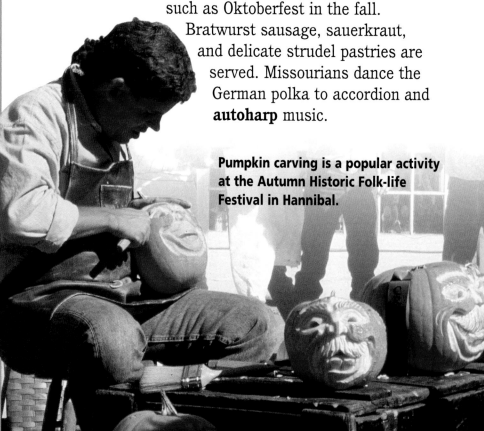

Pumpkin carving is a popular activity at the Autumn Historic Folk-life Festival in Hannibal.

Swing music was developed in Kansas City clubs at the corner of 18th and Vine.

Although many Native Americans were driven out of Missouri by European settlement, a few groups remain. Native-American songs and stories can be heard at various celebrations. Performers gather around a traditional drum, beating a rhythm. They chant and sing the songs of their ancestors, often wearing traditional clothing and jewelry.

Missouri's rich African-American culture is on display in Kansas City in the historic 18th and Vine area. During the early part of the century, this African-American neighborhood produced some of the finest jazz ever recorded. Artists such as Count Basie, John Coltrane, and Charlie Parker have helped to make 18th and Vine a location that is known around the world.

QUICK FACTS

The state's French heritage is celebrated Memorial Day weekend in St. Louis and Ste. Genevieve.

Independence is considered a holy city by the Church of Jesus Christ of Latter-day Saints, or Mormons. The Mormons were eventually forced out of Missouri in what became known as the Mormon War (1836-1839).

The historic Gem Theater was built in 1912 as a movie house for African Americans. The theater now houses the American Museum of Jazz and is only a few steps away from the corner of 18th and Vine.

Mormon Visitor Center

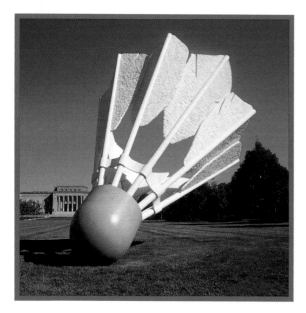

Kansas City's Sculpture Park is home to four 18-foot-tall sculptures of badminton "birdies."

ARTS AND ENTERTAINMENT

While Kansas City is known for its great jazz music, St. Louis is home to some of the best blues music in the country. The blues music scene began in the early part of the twentieth century, when blues musicians from the Mississippi Delta traveled upriver to St. Louis. The sounds of the South mixed with **ragtime** music to create a whole new type of blues known as "St. Louis Blues," named after a song by W. C. Handy.

Missouri is also home to many talented writers. Poets T. S. Eliot and Sara Teasdale were both born in St. Louis. Eliot is considered one of the greatest poets of the twentieth century. Eliot's poem, *The Waste Land*, was a criticism of the society in which he lived. Laura Ingalls Wilder was also from Missouri. She wrote the popular Little House on the Prairie series from her family home in the Ozarks.

Fans of *Little House on the Prairie* can visit the old Rocky Ridge Farm where Laura Ingalls Wilder grew up. Her books were the basis for the television series of the same name.

The North American Aerobatic Team has been delighting audiences at the Air Show of Fair St. Louis for more than 15 years.

QUICK FACTS

The Fair St. Louis, held every fourth of July, is one of the biggest Independence Day celebrations in the country.

Missouri's French heritage is brought to life in many state events. Bastille Days and *Fête d'Automne* are two festivals where French food and entertainment are celebrated.

The Missouri Historical Society displays items relating to the famous Spirit of St. Louis. The aircraft was named in honor of its supporters in St. Louis who paid for the aircraft. The airplane was flown by St. Louis pilot Charles Lindbergh during its historic flight across the Atlantic Ocean.

Josephine Baker was born in St. Louis. Baker is known for bringing African-American jazz and culture to Paris in the 1920s.

Author Mark Twain was also born in Missouri. His well-known book, *The Adventures of Huckleberry Finn*, has made him one of the country's most beloved authors of all-time. Twain also wrote the popular *The Adventures of Tom Sawyer*.

Outdoor entertainment can be found all year long in Missouri. Every July, the town of Hannibal honors Mark Twain with its National Tom Sawyer Days. Popular activities include a fence-painting contest, a "Tom and Becky" look-alike contest, and a frog-jumping contest. The event has been voted one of the best family festivals in the United States, and draws visitors into the city from all over the world. The city of St. Joseph opens its doors to visitors in April to celebrate the birth of the Pony Express and the life of the outlaw Jesse James.

The National Tom Sawyer Days originated in 1956. The event lasts for five days at the beginning of every July.

The Negro Leagues Baseball Museum pays tribute to the great African-American baseball players of the early 1900s.

SPORTS

Missourians, young and old, love sports. The state has a total of five professional sports teams. Baseball enthusiasts watch the St. Louis Cardinals and the Kansas City Royals run the bases. Football season kicks off with the St. Louis Rams and the Kansas City Chiefs. The winter season heats up when the St. Louis Blues hockey team hits the ice. The team has excited fans since 1967, and was named in honor of the city's blues music scene.

Missouri is also home to several sports museums. In 1991, the Negro Leagues Baseball Museum opened in Kansas City. The museum celebrates the history of African-American baseball in the United States. In Springfield, the Missouri Sports Hall of Fame works to recognize and reward the state's great athletes. Recent additions to the hall include Stan Musial and Jack Buck.

QUICK FACTS

Stanley Frank Musial was a popular pitcher for the St. Louis Cardinals. He was known to his fans as "Stan the Man."

Busch Stadium, home of the St. Louis Cardinals, seats 49,676 people.

Arrowhead Stadium, home of the Kansas City Chiefs, held its first game in 1972.

The city of St. Louis was given a National Hockey League (NHL) franchise in 1967.

Arrowhead Stadium

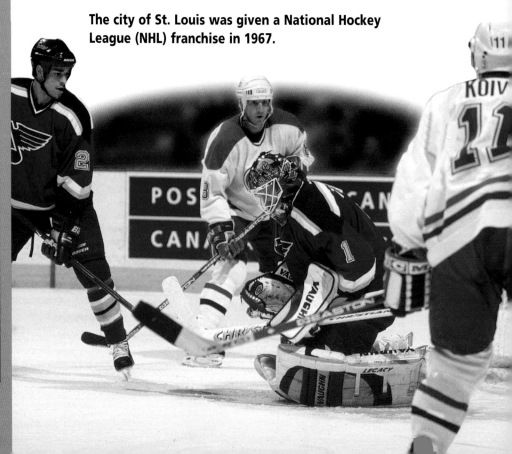

Onondaga Cave is a popular spot for spelunking because of its beautiful rock formations.

Outdoor sports are popular in Missouri. The state's rivers are ideal for canoeing and rafting, while cyclists can take in the 200-mile-long Katy Trail. With over 5,000 caves, **spelunking** is another favorite activity. Some of the more popular caves include Meramec Cavern, hideout of the outlaw Jesse James, and Fantasy World Caverns, which once housed an underground dance hall and skating rink.

Fishing and hunting in Missouri's many lakes, rivers, and forests are common pursuits. Game hunters seek out quail, pheasant, wild turkey, rabbit, and deer. Fishers catch bass, catfish, bluegill, and jack salmon. Float fishing is common in the Ozarks. Fishermen travel down rivers and around lakes, trailing fishing line behind them.

QUICK FACTS

Sportscaster Jack Buck announced baseball games for the St. Louis Cardinals. Whenever the Cardinals won a game Buck would use his trademark phrase—"That's a winner!"

Missouri's Bridal Cave holds the record for the most underground weddings. More than 1,800 couples from around the world have exchanged vows in the cave.

Horse racing is a popular state sport. Interest in horse racing started when people from Virginia and Kentucky first moved to the state, bringing their love of horse racing with them.

Missouri has many fantastic bike paths for cyclists, such as the Katy Trail which runs parallel to the Missouri River.

Brain Teasers

1

Which well-known animator opened his first studio in Kansas City?

Answer: Walter Elias Disney. Walt Disney moved to Kansas City with his family in 1910. He is known for creating Mickey Mouse, Donald Duck, and Disneyland. Disney also produced the first animated movie ever, *Snow White and the Seven Dwarfs*.

2

What was Mark Twain's real name?

Answer: Samuel Langhorne Clemens. He used the pen name Mark Twain when he wrote.

3

Where was the first kindergarten established in the United States ?

Answer: The first kindergarten was established in St. Louis in 1873. The DesPerres School was started by Susan Elizabeth Blow.

4

Which citizen from Missouri once lived in the White House?

Answer: Lamar is the birthplace of Harry S. Truman, the thirty-third president of the United States.

5

Which two foods were invented at the World's Fair in St. Louis in 1904?

Answer: Iced tea and the ice-cream cone were both invented at the 1904 World's Fair.

6

What was the Missouri Compromise?

Answer: In 1818, when Missouri applied for statehood there was controversy over whether they would be admitted as a free state or a slave state. The Missouri Compromise allowed the state to keep its slaves, but placed restrictions on future slave states.

7

Which Missouri city is known for its many boulevards and fountains?

Answer: Kansas City has more boulevards than any city except Paris, and more fountains than any city except Rome.

8

Which well-known scientist was born near Diamond Grove?

Answer: George Washington Carver. Carver overcame a life of slavery to become known around the world as a revolutionary agricultural scientist. His experiments with peanuts convinced southern farmers to plant crops other than cotton.

FOR MORE INFORMATION

Books

Sanford, William R. and Green, Carl R. *America the Beautiful: Missouri*. Chicago: Children's Press, 1990.

Fradin, Dennis Brindell, and Fradin, Judith Bloom. *Missouri*. Chicago: Children's Press, 1994.

Johnson, Cathy. *Missouri: Off the Beaten Path*. Guilford: Globe Pequot Press, 1996.

Hintz, Martin. *America the Beautiful: Missouri*. Second Series. New York: Children's Press, 1999.

Web sites

You can also go online and have a look at the following Web sites:

50 States: Missouri
http://www.50states.com/missouri.htm

Stately Knowledge: Missouri
http://www.ipl.org/youth/stateknow/mo1.html

Missouri Division of Tourism
http://www.missouritourism.org

Missouri Community Web
http://digmo.org/community/arts2.html

Some Web sites stay current longer than others. To find other Missouri Web sites, enter search terms such as "Missouri," "St. Louis," "Kansas City," or any other topic you want to research.

GLOSSARY

abolished: ended

aerospace: aircraft, missiles, and spacecraft

amendments: changes to a law or set of laws

autoharp: string instrument used in folk and country-and-western music

bebop: a style of jazz based on improvisation developed in the 1940s

bluegrass: an early form of country music

charters: documents that set out the rights of an organization or a group of citizens

confluence: the place where two or more rivers join

drainage basin: the area drained by a river

ecosystems: all the elements of an environment and how they interact

extinction: no longer living on Earth

fertile: rich in the nutrients required to grow crops

free state: a state that did not permit slavery

geodesic dome: a light dome structure made out of interlocking surfaces

hydroelectric: related to the creation of energy from moving water

Louisiana Purchase: a large amount of territory purchased from France by the United States in 1803

merged: two companies joined together to make one

ragtime: type of music played mainly on the piano, developed out of African-American folk music

reservations: lands reserved for Native Americans

reservoirs: artificially created bodies of water

riverport: a city or town located on a river, where ships can load and unload

segregation: forced separation and restrictions based on race

slave state: a state that permitted slavery

spelunking: exploring caves and underground caverns

swing: a style of jazz played by a large dance band

terrain: land

INDEX